Singer Songwriter

Singer Songwriter

Alf Taylor

Magabala Books

First published by Magabala Books Aboriginal Corporation
Broome, Western Australia, 1992

Magabala Books receives financial assistance from the Government of
Western Australia, through the Department for the Arts; ATSIC, the
Aboriginal and Torres Strait Islander Commission; and the Australia
Council, the Federal Government's arts funding and advisory body.
Grateful acknowledgement is made for the support of Apple Computer
Australia in the provision of Apple Macintosh equipment.

Editor Peter Bibby
Designer Narelle Jones
Cover artist Miriam Stead
Production Coordinator Donna Ifould
Production Consultant Simon MacDonald
Printed by Frank Daniels, Perth, Western Australia
Typeset in Palatino

National Library of Australia
Cataloguing-in-publication data

Taylor, Alfred, Date.
  Singer Songwriter.

  Includes index.
  ISBN 1 875641 03 3.

  [1.] Aborigines, Australian - Poetry. I. Title.

A821.3

Alf Taylor would like to dedicate this book of poetry to his mother and father, his brother Anthony (deceased) and sisters Madeline and Phyllis (both deceased). He would like to dedicate his book to five little candles which will burn in his heart forever, and for his children who are alive today, who inspired him to put the poems together, Alfred junior and Janice Marie.

He would also like to dedicate this book to his brother Benedict and sisters Mary and Alma, who supported him in his struggle to overcome alcohol, and to his nephews and nieces and their families.

"May they keep their love shining very brightly."

"Alone in a cell" was published by *Phoenix Review*, Department of
English, ANU, Canberra, 1990 ISSN 0819 3600

"We blackfellas" was broadcast on *Millbindi*, 6GWN, March 1991

Special words:

boomer	large male kangaroo
gerbah	(pronounce with soft g, as in *ginger*) alcoholic drink
munnaritj	police
Nyungar	south-west language group

CONTENTS

Introduction

Alf Taylor's poems urged me to look through his gentle words, clearly chosen with care, to scenes beyond experiences, which I could not otherwise have known.

In these poems he speaks as a great lover of life: the love of the loved one; the love of the sunlight, the cool morn and the winds and the sky; the love behind the "Pension Day" indulgences; the missing love of "The Hit" and the painful love for the "Fair Skin Boy".

Each poem is pregnant with human issues and uncompromisingly alive with the innermost feelings that lie hidden in the depths of our breasts. Each poem also demands time to absorb and digest carefully. The poet's strength and simplicity reveals a faith in the people he is one with and his achievement is to interpret their joys and sorrows.

His skill moved me. I am grateful for the privilege of introducing this fresh and compelling work.

Faith Bandler

Black skin

Warm sun on black skin
warm soil under black skin
black skin burns
black skin learns
black skin hangs.

Black skin in fear
black skin can't hear
black skin feel pushed
black skin thinks bush.

Black skin with wine
black skin thinks
life not mine
black skin balance on line.

Ancestors cry from afar
black skin head for bar
black skin feel no pain
black skin drunk again.

Black skin see no tomorrow
black skin head in sorrow
black skin fight
black skin see no right.

Black skin cry
black skin die
black skin no hope
black skin grabs rope.

You are

You are a
cool gentle breeze
on a
hot summer's day.

You are
a warm fire
in the
freezing month
of May,

A warm sun
on a
cool morn,

A trickle
of water
to a
parched throat.

On a
placid lake
you are
a boat.

It is
only me
who could see
in my mind.

Sunlight

Standing
on the
edge of darkness
I just
do not
know
what to do.

People are
beckoning me
from the darkness.
I turn
to see you
standing
in the bright
sunlight.

You are
screaming
my name
as I turn
to run
and to
hold you tight.

Moment of paradise

Stolen glances
fleeting
lock of eyes
moment
of paradise.

No
words spoken
chemistry flow
a smile
hearts
beat wild.

The hit

Cascade
of tears
brain
overflow
with fear.

Tightening
of a syringe
prick
of a needle
rejuvenation begin.

Float
into space
play
amongst the stars.

Flare
of vibrant colours
explodes
in his mind.

Tomorrow
awake
in cold sweat
and sorrow

Screams
and screams
for a needle
and a syringe.

Sleepless nights

Sleepless nights
the storm in my head
I want to cover
rolling of waves
head does not want to discover.

Silently drinking
silently thinking
silent thoughts of sleepless nights.

Darkness wakes the mind
the body does not make a sound
thoughts of yesterday
erupt in volcanic disruption.

Love

Let
Today be fine,
Tomorrow it can rain
as I hold
your warm body
next to mine.

Your lips
are inviting
your skin
so soft and smooth.

Your smile
ever so tender
as your hand
clasped in mine.

I could
drink from your cup
filled so much
with love.

So let it be fine
as you gently
press your lips
to mine.

A love affair

Come on in
Let life begin
Behind closed doors
Let our fantasies soar.

A discreet meeting
Between two adults
A love affair
That should not
Be there.

I was the instigator
You were the participator.
At times I feel
This is not right

So I am going to gently Disappear
From your life
And glide silently
Back to my wife.

She

She was
a single mum
whose life
was shattered
by divorce.

She picked up
the pieces
with a child,
she did not
let her
imagination run wild.

Endless
flow of bills
greeted her
each day

As she
gallantly attempted
to find her way.

The petal

Softly
the rose petal
falls to the ground.
Gentle breeze
tosses it
around and around.

Uneven
cobblestones
tear at its
skin.

Bruised and battered
it starts
to cry.
Caught in the brush
it eventually
dies.

The flats

She left
from here
in quiet despair
never more
to return.

These flats,
she said,
are driving
me mad.

With a bowed
head
she whispers,
Yet leaving
my friends
makes me feel
so sad.

A dream

Shrouded
by the darkness
of the night

Your body so close
I wanted to
hold you tight.

I glanced at your face
it looked aglow
your pouting lips
I wanted
to get to know.

A mist of sadness
engulfed me
as you
got up to go.

I awoke
with a start.
Yet again
it seemed
that you
were only
a dream.

Bring back

Gone is the rainbow
from the sky,
gone is the bird
that can't fly,

Gone is the willow
that can't cry,
gone is the wind
that can't sigh,

Gone is a love
I should have tried.
People I know
are on my side.

I'm fed up
with swimming against the tide,
no longer
am I going to hide.

Break the shackles
from your heart,
Arise with the sun
for a brand new start,

Bring back
the rainbow to the sky,
bring back
the bird that can fly,

Let the wind
make the willow cry
as it rustles the leaves
with a sigh.

Fitzroy bed

I see them
all before me
sitting on
the dry Fitzroy bed.
What if
I make a mistake?
was running through my head.

Eager eyes upon me
as I told
of long ago,
the dark
smiles across their faces
gave me
a pleasant glow.

I talked and talked
until
the hot Fitzroy
sun went down.
When I finished
everyone was clapping
and a few were moving around.

I'll never forget
that day.
It will always
be in my head
how they listen intently
on that dry
Fitzroy bed.

Black child

Little black child
as you play
you seem forgotten.

Forgotten like the stories
your father
used to hear
Forgotten like the spear
as bibles appear.

Forgotten like the elders
who tell
of long, long ago
Forgotten like the people
who still
do not wish to know.

But you
little black child
do not grow up wild.
Listen to the elders
as they tell
of long, long ago.

Look at the spear
as it travels through the air.
Into a young man
you grow.
Look after the elders
with care.

Little black child
if you listen and learn
you will never be forgotten.
Wherever you go
the elders will always know.

Pension day

Good mother all week
dignified she keeps.
Baby feels the change
Pension day in range.

Pretty dress on
she carries baby along.
She knows what they'll say
Today is pension day.

Town alive
with pretty clothes.
Baby knows
as mother goes.

Food will be bought
cheap clothes sought.
Better put money here
gotta have a beer.

Pub is loud
mother look proud.
There'll be dancin
and a lotta romancin.

Sun goin down
baby looks around.
Mother sways
effect of pension day.

Baby cry
mother staggers on by.
See how she sway
end of pension day.

Town

Green leaves on trees,
what I like to see,
wind blowin in my face,
my mind I like to erase
town with no grace.

Shadows of past goin by,
life of stress must start,
brush the cobwebs from your heart.

Looking into life of pain,
being caught in the rain,
reserve full of memories,
town full of gain.

Today's tribe thinking of past,
a yacht with a broken mast,
water comes into the bow.
Pick up a spear
and ask . . . how?

Peace all around,
sits in a humpy,
doesn't make a sound,
picks up a paper
and starts to read:
Russia has taken the lead.

A rifle he hunts prey,
humpy he wants to stay,
highway comin by,
town he must try.
Train noise coming afar,
drives down highway
in his flash car.

Alone in a cell

Here I sit in this darkened cell
my head is so heavy
and my body not well.
Been on the plonk for a month or two
my brain so screwed up
I don't know what to do.

A night alone in this cell I dread
being closed up I may as well be dead.
If only I can live through the night
I'm sure tomorrow's gunna be all right.

As the hours pass by I start to see
the devils and monsters are laughing at me
Why didn't I pay that ten dollar fine?
then these devils and monsters wouldn't be mine.

If I do something real bad
I know all my relations will be sad.
If only they'll open the door
I just can't take it no more.

I look at the towel and it looks like a rope
I've got to get it, my only hope.
Noose around my neck I jump to the floor
I hear the distant noise of a key in the door.

Then a voice so far away
seems like it's coming from yesterday:
Get him down get him down
we've got to bring him round.

I often think back as the years go by
What made me attempt to give that stupid act a try?
May all the spirits of my ancestors above me
guide me through the remaining years of my life.

Kimberley

In my flat
looking
out of
my window

Thinking
of the
Kimberley

Where
my heart
longs
to be

Warm sun
of
ultra violet rays
languishing
in the
misty haze
of those
warm sunny days

Setting sun
of
blood and gold
Stairway
to the moon
longing
to go
back soon.

Words

The embers
of their young hearts
silently glowed
the smile on their faces
clearly showed.

The old fella
told the children
of long time ago.

The children
listen intently
grasping every word.

Dare not
to make a sound
as the words
gently flow
around and around.

My mind

In my mind I see
gold and diamonds surround me,
standing around a shroud
or floating on a cloud.

My mind is my travel agency,
it takes me to any place I fancy,
it makes me write a fancy verse
or lets me explore the Universe.

I really appreciate my mind
when my body's in a bind
with it, I can become King
or with a voice of honey I can sing.

My mind is so free,
I can be what I want to be,
no obstacle too strong,
no road is too long.
In my mind I can do no wrong.

Or when I feel like tossing it in
it makes me fight like hell to win,
it tells me I'm just me.
It always brings me back to reality.

King of the Kimberley

A lack
of understanding
that goes on today,
complete ignorance
in society
I would say.

Aboriginal culture
has to be
taught in schools today.
We were always told
of Captain Cook
sailing on his
merry way.

Even Ned Kelly
in a conversation
always held sway.

Why not talk about Pigeon
in his feats of bold,
always leaving the troopers
standing out
in the cold.

Soldier Pigeon

Soldier
of fortune
Soldier
of fame
Soldier
of the
highest regard
Soldier Pigeon
who rode
the Kimberley Range.

Sniffin

Why
do you sniff glue
they asked?

I don't know
I reply
Maybe I'll forget tomorrow.

In our household
there is
a lot of sorrow,

Nan is sick
Mum cannot cope
and Dad
he is drunk again.

I have
got so little space
and yet
so much time,

I sometimes wish
this life
not mine.

I wish I had
a lotta schoolin
then
this stupid sniffing
I won't be doin.

So I will
probably sniff glue again
to get away
from that shadow
of pain.

The trip

Lifting the bottle
to his parched lips
the revolting liquid
his hungry throat
did not want to miss.

With a grunt and a groan
into an empty well
the dirty brown liquid
fell like a stone.

The warmth in his blood
started to flow
eyes glazed
words become slow

Floating into universe
warm sun explodes
into a cascade of brilliance
of flowing fun.

Where did I go wrong?
he gently weeps
resting his head
on the evening star
as he goes into a blissful sleep.

Dole cheque

Dole cheque comes today
I wish that I could steal away
all the Nyungars will be around
gotta get away without making a sound.

Nyungars will head to the pub
that's where they'll find me
sitting quietly here
having a beer.

They'll be asking for a price
I'll give but it won't be nice
cheques don't last long today
I may as well give or they won't go away.

Grab a carton and a flagon
and head for the bush
before the Munnaritj
give us the push.

A drunken voice will say
"Hey that's not right,
you got my woman.
Me and you gonna fight."

Sun comes up bodies go down
black eyes and love bites
as I look around
holding my head in pain
I can't wait for the dole cheque again.

No names

The chains
of silence
have been
broken

By a
Death
in Custody
the word
has been
spoken.

Who is
to blame?
Who is
to blame?
Lots of questions
but no names.

Is it
a game?
No one
is to blame.
A lot
of questions
but still no name.

Lightning Man

Lightning Man strike your light
Across the darkness of the night,
Lightning Man let me hear you
Crack with old man thunder,
Lightning Man please listen to what
I have to say.

Lightning Man along with your clouds
Bring relief to this parched land,
Lightning Man beat the clouds into submission,

Lightning Man make them weep, weep and weep,
Lightning Man so electrifying so strong,
Lightning Man to me you can do no wrong.
Thank you for the tears of rain.

Makin it right

I'll try and make things right
through writing and poetry
I just might
but we'll all have to pull together.
Never mind how far apart
someone somewhere gotta make a start.

With all this bickering amongst black and white
character assassination gives me a fright
if we can't say anything nice to each other
let's not talk, then it's no bother.

When I was a kid there was no colour.
As I got older I found there's black white and yellow.
Who cares about the colour?
It's the person inside that matters.

Let's stop calling each other names,
get into a huddle and start playing the game.
There's only one thing for me
it's winning and winning and being free.

I know that's only a dream of me and you
but if we put our heads together it could come true.
Never mind how far apart
someone somewhere gotta make a start.

Old Blue

I looked down at him,
yes he was getting old.
No more catching roos, I said.
Old Blue dropped his head.

When he was a pup
by his graceful motions
Dad could tell
that he was going to kill well.

When Dad took him out
Mum would make a damper,
knowing in her heart
Old Bluey would kill from the start.

When food was scarce
Old Bluey would provide.
We could see when he'd killed a big boomer
by the scratches on his hide.

As spotlights and rifles began to stalk the prey
Dad would always say,
Give me a good roo dog any day.

High powered cars and bikes,
Old Blue gradually lost his bite
but to us he was always our shining light.

One morning we found that Old Blue had passed on by.
At times our family would cry
for a wonderful roo dog somewhere in the sky.

Debbil Man

The Debbil Man
I see
in the darkness
is beckoning me.
Come . . . come
I hear
the chilly night wind calling.

I know
what the tribe
will say: Keep away, keep away,
for him bad.
You go to him
we all be sad.

They say
he will
take your spirit
your body and your soul.

He Debbil Man
that one, pull blanket
over
your head.
And don't listen
to what
the Debbil Man
said.

The mission

After prayers at night I go to bed
lying awake with memories in my head.
I can still see my mother kneeling on the ground
sobbing, Don't take my child, I want him around,

When the Native Welfare came and took me away.
Even now at times I still cry inwards and say
I belong to a tribe, honest and just,
not a religion, we live by a must.

Not in a mission, but I'd rather be
hugging my mother, sitting on her warm bended knees.
For one day I'd like to tell the world
how the missionaries put my brain in a whirl.

I tried my best to play along with their rules
praying and praying and going to school.
Being a blackfella was my only tool,
doing things for Jesus and keeping my cool.

I know one day I'll be free,
free from religion and free from rules.
Free to make up my own mind and free to be cool
but I know the damage has already been done
as I see myself lying drunk in the hot morning sun.

Rules

I looked
at the figure
before me

It was dishevelled
and trembling slightly.
The cracks
on his face
I would have
loved to erase.
Death was approaching
but he
did not want me
to know.

With a quiver
in his voice
he turned to me
and said,

Once boy
our ancestors
were free
in this beautiful land.
Now
I don't understand.
So many rules so many rules
blackfellas
owning the jails
still cannot own land.

With tears
in my eyes
I watched
him shuffle away.
Looking
at his bent back,
I openly cried
and whispered
I love you Dad.

Goodbye.

In memory of Kevin "Doc" Humphries

from Alma

Oh Doc
I can see the darkness
on a bright sunny day
since you
were laid to rest
on that hot summer's day.

I can still see your coffin
being lowered down.
My heart openly wept
knowing you will
never be around.

You was
a gun shearer
in the past
until gerbah
took its toll.
I felt you would not last.

Now I look back
on the good times we had.
With you away shearing
I always felt sad.

When you
got back to the camp
it was always great.
With pound notes
in your hand

you would grab and kiss me
saying, "Here you are mate!"

You used
to keep me awake
playing Slim Dusty's tapes
ever so loudly.
You would listen
to them proudly.

Now
I feel like a shell
but I still
got my memories
of you, dear Doc.

Fight

Had to fight since the day I was born
on that cold winter morn,
not only for life but for dignity
in today's society.

I had to fight every inch of the way
to get where I am today
around drunken fights
surrounded by drunken nights.

Dole cheque every fortnight
was my only shining light
but after long last
I really was going nowhere fast.

Put myself in gear
decided to get away from here
fed up with drunken nights
headed for the city lights.

Not quite grasping the straw
with determination I pushed for more.
Support from friends was overwhelming
sunlight was just beginning.

Fair skin boy

Wrenching
of a heart,
killing
of joy,
being parted
from her
fair skin boy.

Agonising years
river of tears
emptiness
all around.

Lived
with hope
one day
she will
see
her fair skin boy.

Chance
on a street
she did meet
her fair skin boy.

Mother

My dear kind, sweet and loving Mum

I can't understand why
for such a gentle woman to pass on by.
I always thought you would live forever
I thought, death to you never.

I know roses bloom then die
I know the grass go brown with no rain
but when they told me that you died
all I felt was pain.

So farewell and not goodbye Mum
Your body is gone but not your spirit.
My love for you will be shouted aloud
so wherever you are you will hear it.

I feel your presence all around
and sometimes I feel it on the ground.
Your patience, love and understanding,
your rules never hard and demanding.

I will leave your freshly mounded grave
knowing all your life you gave.
In my heart there is no other
only the memory of you dear Mother.

The fine

He talked
about the time
when the police
picked him up
for a lousy fine.

Ten dollars fifty he said
as he
unintelligently scratched
his head.

Locked away
with murderers, rapists,
child abusers
and bum bandits.

When the time
was up
they unlocked the door.
He went so fast
the coppers never
seen him no more.

A price

He told me
when he was a young boy
he was always
on the roam
never quite stayed
in one place
long enough
to call it home.

Cheap wine
and a park bench
was his only
gift to life.
Maybe, he said,
things might
have been different
if
I would have
taken a wife.

But I am
too old now
to worry about the past
I just live
for today,
tomorrow can take care
of itself.

So please
give me a price my friend
cause I do not care
if my life
is at an end.

No hope

I have
seen it before
and I see it now.
How far will it go
before
someone walks through
the door?

The haze
of alcohol
lingers in the air.
The smell of
sweaty bodies
and the stench
of dope.
These are the people
of no life
and no hope.

Last ride

Neon lights
were beckoning him
as he hit
the street that night.

Little did he know
what was in store.
He would never be
patrolling the streets
no more.

His friends
in a stolen car
pulled up.
Jump in, they yelled,
we're going for a spin.

Drinks in the car
as neon lights
flashed past.
They heard the wailing sound
of sirens at last.

Thrill
of the chase
power of the car
police beaten by far.

Driver
not realising
he was at a bend on a hill.

Crunch
of twisted metal
then everything was still
for all five teenagers
in the stolen car were killed.

Gerbah

People on gerbah going nowhere fast
think people don't drink are coming last.
Little they know these people who go slow
always sure of knowing just where they go.

I heard him say, with drunken pride,
Tellin me gerbah no good they gotta hide,
tellin me about gerbah. I'm a man.
No one tells me, I'll drink all I can.

Today he'll enjoy life and have all the fun.
The time he's forty body wrecked his life nearly done.
Dead brain cells and a burnt out liver,
lays in a cold sweat and starts to shiver.

Lying in a hospital doctors all around
Why didn't I listen? he thinks. He doesn't make a sound
When I was younger should've slowed down a pace.
No-use cryin I think I've run my race.

Message Mum gets, he has died today
She's upset and quite dismayed.
Why didn't my boy slowen down, she sobs,
Not drinkin around with all his mob?

With no schoolin what have they got?
A dole cheque and a bottle, that's what.
Schoolin is a must for today
For the kids so that they can help pave the way.

We blackfellas

We say there is hope for tomorrow
but we blackfellas
are still living in sorrow.
We are trying to make a life.
The media always keeps us in strife.

Never of good things
we do.
The media will always punish
me and you.

We blackfellas are trying
to stand tall.
Our enemy the media
are always making us fall.

We have been stripped
of our pride.
The media have got a hide.
We blackfellas must stand
as one
as the fight still goes on.

'88

With Prince Charles opening the year
the blackfella still living in fear,
I can understand all the fuss it caused
'88 I look back on with remorse.

Black Deaths in Custody was the main topic.
The man at the top said he was going to stop it.
More money was the order of the day,
this giving the authorities more power to flay.

Bombing and killing were oh so ripe,
bank robbers making their daily swipe,
drugs and prostitution was always a point,
kids roamin the street sucking a joint.

Deaths on roads were oh so frequent,
with random breath testing they tried to end it
but faster the car the deadlier the weapon
as another mangled wreck lay out in the open.

Death and destruction number one of the year,
another woman raped, bashed and living in fear.
With hunger pains in its belly, the little child
screams in mother's ear
as mums and dads quietly shed a tear.

I just hope things are different in '99
as we all advance hand in hand in an horizontal line.
Maybe if we all prayed to the almighty above
to give those two terrible Ds a shove.

Wall of darkness

Feel safe
within the wall of darkness.
No one
can touch me
no one can see,
only me.

I see a tribe
who's solemn and sad.
I see infighting,
it make's me feel so bad.

I see my ancestors
rise from the dead
so proud
so strong
the chains
around their necks
so heavy, so long.

Across their chest
is a message
written in blood:

We died
that you could live
we died
that you could give.
Leave the bottle alone
if not
the lizards
will leave only bone.

Then I see
the spirit of my mother
looking for me.

Her face
has a saintly glow
she is at peace
and she knows

No more
being torn apart
by her fair skin
from the start.

I have
got to come out
from this wall of darkness

Where people can see,
people can touch me.
I won't accept it
but I have to
come back to reality.

Dreams

Oh for the dreams
l had last night
some were scary
some were bright.

I dreamt I held your hand
but I couldn't understand
that your hair was red
and your body dead.

You floated above me
you told me you loved me
you looked like the morning star
shining from afar.

Then I dreamt we slept in a bed of roses.
People said they didn't know us.
I'm sure I was the King
laying without the Queen.

I didn't want to surrender to the dawn
as I awoke to the chill of the morn,
laid back and tried to capture that dream.
Not likely it seems.

Leave us alone

I wish these do-gooders would leave us alone
for we have been forty thousand years on our own.
Stop leading us blackfellas around,
we want our two feet firmly on the ground.

Religion and missions have really screwed us up.
I don't know who's black and who's not,
black preachers telling us the Lord is the lot
but I know the whitefella gives cold beer when it's hot.

I know the government gives you money to sit down.
Why work when you can go drinking around
but there's only one thing I'd like to see
is stopping black deaths in custody.

Today I see a tribe who's uneasy and sad
the do-gooders don't know it but they're driving us mad.
Education is a must for today,
our tribal customs must always stay.

It's dog eat dog in this world today,
killer instinct we must develop and make it stay.
Challenge problems, not running away,
forget about the booze and family fights,
let's stand up as individuals and make it right.

So back off and give me some space,
it's gonna be me running this race.
So please leave us alone
I'd like to be left on my own.

Elders

Look
at the elders
as they
talk
with their hands.

They are
like trees
in
our beautiful land.

Listen
to the elders
as they tell
of
long time ago.

Watch
the elders
as they
take aim
with their spear.

For they
are like
the Kimberley rains
so far
yet so near.

Let's

The children
are men and women
of tomorrow.
Let's look after
mother earth
so they won't be
burdened with sorrow.

Let the trees
reach for the heavens.
Let the sand
move with the tide.
Let the
children have fun.
Let's protect the ozone layer
so our children
won't have to hide
from the midday sun.

New beginning

Sliding
down rainbows,
chasing moonbeams,
tranquility and serenity,
life is so happy
it seems.

Cool rain
cascading
on parched land,
blustery winds,
the moving sands.

Life is wonderful,
we can understand
smiling faces.
Life is not over,
new beginning
because – we're sober.

Index of titles

Index of first lines